BY SEA TO
AMERICA

Brian Moses
Illustrated by Tom McNeely

A Harcourt Achieve Imprint

www.Rigby.com
1-800-531-5015

CHAPTER ONE

TRAIN RIDE

Anya Sakowicz groaned. She knew what her little brother Micah was going to ask before he even opened his mouth.

"Are we nearly there yet?"

Anya tried her best to keep reading and ignore him.

It had been February when they'd left their home in Poland, and now it was March. Anya busied herself with reading and keeping a diary. She'd lost count of how many trains they'd taken west from Poland to England, but she reminded herself that every day brought her closer to her father.

Like many people from Poland, Jakub Sakowicz, Anya's father, had left over a year ago to look for work in America. Before long Jakub had saved enough money to buy the tickets that would bring his family to join him.

This train would take them to Liverpool, a port city on the west coast of England. There they would board a ship that would take them across the Atlantic Ocean to their new home.

"Are we nearly there *yet*?" Micah asked.

Anya heard her mother Klaudia say, "I know it's hard. At only eight years old, we're taking you away from everything you've ever known."

Leaving Poland had been hard for Anya, too. She'd grown up in a small village and now, just after her 12th birthday, her whole life was being turned upside down. She wondered why they'd had to leave. Life hadn't been easy, she knew that, but everyone in the village had struggled. Some weeks there was enough food, and at other times they went hungry.

"Things will be better in America," Klaudia had told her. "America is a Golden Land."

The next day the Sakowicz family arrived in Liverpool, where they found a grand ship waiting for them at the dock. It was the largest thing Anya had ever seen. It was so long that she almost wasn't able to see the end of it, and it had four smoke stacks coming out of the top. Anya's mouth fell open in amazement.

"This is the RMS *Lusitania*," Klaudia said. "That sounds like a fine name, don't you think?"

For five days they waited to board the ship, sleeping in a small hotel room at night, and filling out endless paperwork during the day. Each day they had to find someone who could speak Polish and translate for them.

Then there were the examinations. Everyone had to be checked out by a doctor, and nearly everyone—including Anya—was given painful shots.

When everything was in order, they collected the third-class tickets Anya's father had bought for them, and they were finally taken on board the *Lusitania*.

CHAPTER TWO

GETTING SETTLED

There was a lot of cheering and clapping as the *Lusitania* slowly sailed away from the dock. It was strange to feel the ship moving, and Anya grabbed the handrail for support.

The crowds on the dock waved and cried out *goodbye*! Those on the ship waved back just as excitedly. While most of the passengers were delighted to be leaving, there were tears on some people's faces. Anya guessed that maybe they were leaving their homes behind, which made them sad, or lonely. She felt the same way at times.

There was no one for her brother Micah to wave to, but he waved anyway. Klaudia laughed and waved as well.

When Anya waved, however, she wasn't waving to just anybody—she was waving goodbye to all of Europe.

The decks were crowded, and as they made their way to their cabin, Anya held tightly to her mother's hand.

There were people from many different countries on board, speaking many unfamiliar languages. Some people wore expensive suits and dresses. One woman wore an emerald-colored hat with plumes of red feathers shooting out the top. A group of servants carried the mountain of suitcases she'd brought along.

Others were not so well-dressed, yet they, like Anya and her family, seemed the most excited to be setting sail.

Anya wondered if there would be other families from Poland on this ship. She would have to listen carefully everywhere she went to see if she recognized the Polish language being spoken.

It was a long walk along passageways
and down staircases to their tiny cabin
deep within the ship. There they found
metal bunk beds against each wall, a steel
wash basin, and one folding chair. A tiny
porthole looked out onto the sway of the
ocean.

The three of them struggled to get their bags into the small room, bumping knees and elbows. The luggage had to be pushed under the beds or there wouldn't be room to move.

"I'm not sure whether this is cozy or cramped," Klaudia muttered.

Micah bounced up and down on the top bunk. "I'm hungry. When do we eat?"

The third-class dining room had tables and long, wooden benches but hardly any spaces left to sit. The noise of conversation roared through the room. Soup was served, along with herring and potatoes.

The old woman sitting next to Anya coughed into the sleeve of her dress. Anya noticed her mother watching the old woman worriedly. When someone whispered the word *tuberculosis*, Klaudia snatched her children up and their dinner was finished.

ANYA'S PLAN

Anya loved their first evening on the *Lusitania*. Everywhere she looked, she could see groups of passengers talking and laughing, or huddled close together playing cards.

There were people of different ages singing, clapping, and dancing as all sorts of musical instruments were being played. She heard the sound of pipes, a fiddle, an accordion, and several tin whistles. The dancers clapped merrily and stomped their feet in time with the music.

Anya and Micah joined in the fun, hooking arms and twirling each other around and around. She didn't know the song, but she still had a great time.

Everyone seemed relaxed and happy. They were on board at last and sailing to the Golden Land, America.

That night the wind blasted the side of the boat, rocking it in the ocean waters. Anya felt the cabin tip back and forth, and Micah almost rolled out of bed.

Klaudia did not like the movement of the ship. She felt sick, especially if she tried to stand.

"Will Mother be all right?" asked Micah.

"I'm sure she will," Anya replied. "Let's bring her something for breakfast."

When they reached the dining hall, they were disappointed to see that breakfast was herring and potatoes—not the sorts of things to settle a sick stomach.

On the way back to their cabin, the children passed the dining room for first-class passengers. Eggs, bacon, sausages, tomatoes, bread, jam, and fruit of every kind covered the tables.

"We'd find something in there that Mother would enjoy," Anya whispered.

The sun that afternoon was wonderfully warm, and the ocean air smelled clean and salty. Anya and Micah had a wonderful time playing hide-and-seek with the other children on deck. Anya found great hiding places: a broom closet, an empty barrel, and behind a staircase.

At one point, Anya hid behind a stack of deck chairs. She giggled as Micah passed by without seeing her. But then she overheard some adults speaking in Polish.

"You know the rules about Ellis Island," one man said. "The doctor has to check everyone out. If you look sick, they send you back to Europe."

Another man said, "I heard they call it the 'Island of Tears' because so many families are turned away."

"Mother," Anya whispered, fearing the worst. She rushed off to find her brother.

The next morning, Klaudia looked even worse. Anya thought it would help if she tried to eat something.

Breakfast was porridge and milk, which Klaudia refused to eat. But Anya had a plan to get her mother something better.

Waiting near the first-class dining room, she spoke softly to Micah. "Keep watch for me. I'm going to get some of that bread for Mother."

Anya knew her mother had always enjoyed warm bread and fresh butter, so she would do her best to get her some.

She took one step toward the food, then a voice stopped her in her tracks.

"I really wouldn't do that if I were you."

Anya spun around to find a white-haired gentleman towering over her.

CHAPTER FOUR

MR. KRINSKY

"I'm sorry, sir!" Anya answered, rather frightened. "I would never steal, but you see, my mother's ill and needs to eat."

"I'm sorry to hear that," the man replied back to her in Polish, her native language. "But if you're caught, they'll lock you up as a thief, then send you back to Europe."

"I'm very sorry. Please don't tell on me," said Anya.

"I won't tell anyone anything. You see, I'm also Polish," the man said, smiling a kind smile. "My name is Bendek Krinsky. Tell me your cabin number, and I'll bring some food for your mother."

Anya gave him the number. "And thank you, sir!" she cried as she bolted down the hallway.

"Oh, and my name's Anya!"

A short time later, Mr. Krinsky knocked on their door, holding a plate of food and a pitcher of water for Anya's mother.

"Good day, madam. I hear you are unwell. Might I tempt you with a little breakfast? There's fresh bread here."

"That's very kind of you, sir," Klaudia replied, smiling.

As Anya's mother ate, they discussed Poland, their homeland. For many generations, the Sakowicz family had lived in the village of Trawniki. Mr. Krinsky knew of that village. When they told him their family name, he clapped his hands with joy.

"I knew your grandfather, Henryk Sakowicz. We served in the army together," he said. "Your grandfather was a great man and dear to my heart. I'll never forget the kindness he showed me."

Mr. Krinsky stayed and talked for a while longer. Then he advised Klaudia to rest. She had eaten a good breakfast, her first in several days.

Anya helped gather the dirty dishes. As Mr. Krinsky was leaving, he whispered to Anya, "I'll get the ship's doctor to pay your mother a visit. See that she rests as much as she can."

But Anya was worried. They had no spare money to pay for a doctor. They had brought all they had—a few *grosz*—but it wasn't much. There were still many expenses for the family to cover before they reached America.

Anya needn't have worried. When the doctor arrived with pills to take away the seasickness, he said there was no charge.

"Mr. Krinsky has already paid me," explained the doctor.

The medicine was a great help. Klaudia grew stronger and stronger over the next few days and began eating regularly. Mr. Krinsky stopped by the cabin now and again to check up on them. Anya asked him to stay and tell her stories about her grandfather Henryk fighting in the Polish army.

As it turned out, most of the adults traveling third class were seasick as well, while the children were seldom bothered by it.

"We had the whole dining room all to ourselves," Anya told her mother. "The staff served tables full of children. It was very funny."

The food in third class was still the same though. There was potatoes, soup, cold biscuits, and only a little meat. But the children were usually so hungry, they ate whatever they were given.

One morning Micah came crashing through the cabin door. "Anya!" he shouted. "Anya, come at once!"

"Why? What's the matter?"

"There's a whale, a really big whale, and it's right alongside the ship. Come and look!"

They raced along passageways and climbed staircases until they reached the upper deck. A huge crowd had lined up along the ship's railings and was peering out into the water. It was hard to find a space in the crowd to see, but eventually two of the crew let them squeeze through.

The ocean air was chilled and damp that morning, and Anya felt the cold sink into her bones. In all the rush and excitement, she'd forgotten her coat.

"Where is it? Where is the whale?" Anya asked. A moment later, a fit of coughing struck her, and she had to cover her mouth.

"There it is!" Micah cried.

The children stared in amazement. The huge creature was keeping pace with the ship, and every now and then a fountain of water spouted up from its head.

The whale opened its mouth, and a wave of white-crested water disappeared inside. Its skin was gray and wrinkly. Anya had read the story of *Jonah and the Whale* and wondered if there was a tiny boat lost in the belly of this whale.

Then Micah pointed excitedly. "Look! There's another one! Do you see it?"

A second whale broke through the surface, blew a spray of water up into the air, then dove back under.

"They're beautiful," Anya said.

Another coughing fit came over her then, and Anya had to brace herself against her brother.

"Anya! Where is your coat?"

It was their mother, out of bed for the first time in a week. She knelt beside her daughter, feeling her chest as she coughed. She felt Anya's forehead and cheek, then stood and took her hand.

"Come back inside. You'll catch your death of cold out here."

Anya continued to cough as her mother led her to the stairs. She noticed that people were staring at her. One woman backed away, pressing a handkerchief to her mouth. She leaned over to the woman next to her and whispered *tuberculosis*.

Klaudia rushed her daughter downstairs out of the cold ocean air.

CHAPTER FIVE

ILLNESS AND INJURY

Anya's cough grew worse. It kept her up at night, and without proper rest, she soon developed a fever.

Mr. Krinsky called for the ship's doctor once more. The doctor listened to Anya's chest with a stethoscope, took her pulse, and flashed a light into her eyes.

In the end, Anya was given a cough remedy and told to stay in bed. The medicine tasted horrible, and she felt sick every time she swallowed it. She wouldn't have minded the taste so much if she felt the medicine were doing her any good, but the cough seemed to bother her all the time now.

Anya read and wrote in her diary, but it was boring staying in bed all day.

Things weren't going so well for Micah, either. One afternoon he came limping into their cabin. His arm was slung around the shoulders of another boy, who set him down and then rushed out.

"Micah," Klaudia scolded, "what did you do?"

Micah explained that he'd been having foot races with some of the other boys up and down the decks when his foot caught a rope cable attached to a stack of life preservers.

"But I won three races before I fell!" Micah said proudly.

His ankle was red and swollen, but since he was able to put some weight on it, Klaudia didn't think it was broken. She tore a blouse into long strips and bound his ankle tightly.

As the *Lusitania* approached America's shores, Anya could tell her mother was getting nervous. Both of her children were laid up in bed—one with a bad cough, the other with an injured ankle.

What would the doctors do if Anya and Micah failed the medical exams? Would they still be able to see their father?

Anya tried not to think about it. She sipped some water to calm her cough, then crawled back into bed.

Klaudia sat on the edge of Anya's bed and sang a Polish lullaby until her daughter was asleep.

Hotch urody nie mam,
Myuntku nieviele.
E tak vas, nie prosche.
O neets pshayiachele.

Though I own a few things,
I'll not ever need more.
I have you, my darling.
You are what I've hoped for.

CHAPTER SIX

ELLIS ISLAND

Just before 6 A.M., there was a lot of noise outside their cabin and the sound of many feet hurrying past.

"It's America!" someone shouted. "Come and look!"

The family dressed and joined a line of passengers snaking their way upstairs to the decks. As they arrived on deck, they could hear cheering.

"It's the lady with the torch," Klaudia said. "It's the Statue of Liberty. We really are in America now!"

Anya felt a mixture of emotions as she saw the huge statue. She felt excitement because her father was somewhere on the island, waiting for her. But she also understood that there were still many challenges to come before she could see her father again.

Anya had never witnessed such a busy scene. New York Harbor was overflowing with activity. There were other ships as big as theirs waiting to dock, with tugboats bobbing around them. She watched the little boats helping to direct the ships into channels marked by floating buoys. There were also many large sailing ships with cream-colored sails billowing out like clouds.

Hundreds of workers hurried around on the docks. Whistles blew and flags of all colors waved through the air. Anya had no idea what it all meant, but it was lovely to watch.

Eventually around midday, it was the *Lusitania's* turn to dock.

"Here we are, children," Klaudia said, taking both their hands. "Let's go and pack our things. We'll be onshore soon."

After they were packed, the Sakowicz family watched the first-class passengers leave the ship. Those passengers were lucky since they'd been given their medical exams onboard the ship.

For the third-class passengers, it would be a different welcome. Klaudia had spoken to Micah about trying hard not to limp. She had also spoken to Anya, but if her daughter tried not to cough it only seemed to make matters worse. The last thing they wanted was for Anya to have a coughing fit as they were waiting to be examined.

The third-class passengers were led off the ship and loaded onto boats for the short trip across New York Harbor to Ellis Island. Anya guessed that there were about two hundred people on their boat. Most of them were standing, as there were few seats. She noticed that she was trembling, but she didn't want her mother to realize how frightened she was. She coughed quietly into her handkerchief.

"Keep close to me at all times," Klaudia told them. "And behave well. We don't want to draw attention to ourselves in any way."

Anya looked around as they left the boat. They were joining the end of a long line of people waiting to enter a large building. She felt hungry. They hadn't eaten since breakfast, so she was pleased to find that food was being given out as they waited. There was brown bread with sardines, cheese, and milk or coffee to drink.

All around commands were being shouted in a language that the family didn't understand. Then slowly, very slowly, the line began to move forward.

Anya was trying hard not to cough. She knew that her mother was scared from the tight way in which she gripped her hand. How awful it would be to get so far and then be sent back!

The line of people shuffled along until at last they entered the building. There they discovered a great hall filled with baggage of all kinds. They were given labels for their bags, which were then added to the pile. Anya wondered whether they'd ever find their bags again among all the confusion.

CHAPTER SEVEN

THE AMERICAN DOCTORS

Next they joined another line that also moved very, very slowly. Klaudia held Anya's and Micah's hands the entire time.

The line went up a steep flight of stairs to the second floor of a huge building. Many of those traveling on the ship were here in line, and everyone looked nervous.

Inside the crowd of people were made to walk single file through a roped maze that wound back and forth, back and forth.

At the end of the line, a team of doctors inspected people as they passed by. Anya watched Micah trying hard not to limp. She could see the pain on his face as he placed his hurt foot on the floor.

Two of the doctors passed Micah without looking twice. Then suddenly, a third doctor reached out and drew a blue chalk mark *L* on Micah's back. Then the doctor moved on to the next person in line.

Anya heard her mother gasp. "Please, no! Have mercy on us."

The shock of seeing her brother marked in this way set Anya to coughing. She couldn't stop herself. She held on to her mother until she was able to catch her breath again. Another doctor stepped toward her, and a blue *T* was chalked on Anya's back.

Anya's heart sank into her stomach. A tear escaped her eye and rolled down her cheek.

"What will they do with us? Please don't let them send us back," Klaudia said quietly.

A man in uniform directed them into a smaller room filled with people. All of these people had blue marks chalked on their backs, too. Everyone looked worried, and no one spoke very much at all.

Anya and Micah held on tightly to their mother as they waited. Through the high windows, they watched the afternoon pass into evening. Eventually, everyone was led out of the small room and taken into a large room full of beds. Anya and her family had been moved to so many rooms, she had no idea where she was anymore.

They were served a simple meal, then Klaudia prepared her children for bed, though neither of them felt very sleepy.

Suddenly, they heard someone speaking Polish. "Sakowicz? Please, I'm looking for Mrs. Jakub Sakowicz."

Anya knew she recognized the voice. "Mother, look! It's Mr. Krinsky!"

Klaudia raised her hand, and Anya saw her eyes light up. Once again, there was the white-haired gentleman who had been so kind to them on the ship. He came toward them. Surely he could do something!

"Please, Mr. Krinsky," Klaudia said. "The doctors have marked the children. Is there nothing you can do? Don't let them send us back."

"I'm doing everything that I can," Mr. Krinsky answered. "But please don't give up hope. I work for the Polish Society, which helps people from Poland enter America. I know there's nothing wrong with the children, but the doctors need convincing."

"I am sorry that you have to spend the night here," Mr. Krinsky told them. "But please, make yourselves as comfortable as you can, and I will try to visit again after breakfast tomorrow."

"Thank you," Klaudia said, taking his hand in both of hers. "You have been a dear friend to us."

Mr. Krinsky smiled. "Henryk Sakowicz saved my life once," he said.

They slept very little that night. Anya coughed constantly and was sure she kept everyone awake. She thought about her father. Did he know what was happening to them? He must be terribly worried. What would he do if his family was sent home?

Anya could hear her mother crying softly in the next bed. She so wanted her mother to hold her and tell her that everything would be all right.

CHAPTER EIGHT
REUNION

Anya's mother was far from certain that everything would be all right. She had heard too many stories on the voyage over. People were turned away for the slightest of reasons. Those unfortunate souls had to remain at Ellis Island until a ship could be found to take them back to Europe.

Morning could not come fast enough, even if they were fearful of what might happen. At dawn they were given breakfast, and soon afterward, Mr. Krinsky visited them again.

"Try not to worry. I'm sure that everything will be all right," he said. After a long wait, the family was taken to another room where a doctor examined Micah's ankle.

It seemed like hours before the doctor spoke to a man at his side. This man was an interpreter who translated the doctor's words from English into Polish.

"The doctor says he can't find anything permanently wrong with your son's foot. He believes that your son has only sprained it. It should return to normal in a week or so."

Anya realized that she had been holding her breath while the man spoke. She now breathed a sigh of relief and gave her brother a weak smile.

"As for your daughter," the interpreter began, "the doctor doesn't like the sound of her cough."

The doctor peered into Anya's mouth. He muttered once or twice and wrote something down on paper. The interpreter looked on, but said nothing.

The doctor asked Anya to cough and then spit onto a cloth. He asked her to stand up straight while he looked at her spine. He shook his head and spoke to the interpreter.

Anya had heard a horrible word twice on the ship—*tuberculosis*. Would she hear it a third time?

"I'm afraid he is still not satisfied," the interpreter said. "He wants to check with another doctor."

The doctor left the room, and Anya's mother hugged her children tightly. No matter what happened, Anya knew they would not be separated. Even if she was not allowed into America, they would go back to Europe as a family.

Finally the doctor returned. He handed the interpreter some folded papers, then left the room.

Anya's stomach was in her throat until the interpreter smiled and said, "Your daughter has a virus, nothing more. The doctors see no reason why she shouldn't be allowed through."

The interpreter handed Klaudia the papers. "Welcome to America."

The Sakowicz family cheered and cried and laughed and hugged each other tightly. They had made it to America! They had made it to their new home!

Her heart beating fast in her chest, Anya and her family walked out into the sunshine pouring down on New York City.

"Anya! Micah!" a familiar voice called out to them.

Anya turned to see her father pushing through the crowd toward them, and in the next moment, the whole family was together again.

Jakub Sakowicz scooped his two children up into his arms and held them tightly. Somehow he still found room to hug his wife Klaudia as well. They had come so far, and Anya had been afraid this day would never come.

"Oh, Father!" she cried. "I was so worried that I would never see you again. I got a cough on the ship, and the doctors put a blue mark on me, and a very nice man named Mr. Krinsky helped us through it all! I wish I knew where he was so I could thank him!"

Just then, another familiar face pushed through the crowd. It was Mr. Krinsky! After he was introduced to Anya's father, Jakub shook Mr. Krinsky's hand excitedly.

"I have so much to thank you for," Jakub said. "You brought me my family."

"No thanks are necessary," said Mr. Krinsky. "Your father was a good friend to me, Mr. Sakowicz, and it does my heart good to see a family reunited."

"Please, Mr. Krinsky," Klaudia said. "There must be some way that we can repay you."

"Well let's see," Mr. Krinsky scratched his chin. "I would never say no to a fine plate of Polish *kielbasa*!"

"It will be the best you've ever tasted,"
Anya promised, just before giving
Mr. Krinsky the biggest hug she could.